COUTURE CUPCAKES

ERIC LANLARD & PATRICK COX